FORCES

Physical Science for Kids

ANDI DIEHN

Illustrated by Shululu

Nomad Press
A division of Nomad Communications
10 9 8 7 6 5 4 3 2 1

This book was manufactured by CGB Printers,
North Mankato, Minnesota, United States
March 2018, Job #240599

ISBN Softcover: 978-1-61930-638-7
ISBN Hardcover: 978-1-61930-636-3

Educational Consultant, Marla Conn

Questions regarding the ordering of this book should be addressed to
Nomad Press
2456 Christian St.
White River Junction, VT 05001
www.nomadpress.net

Printed in the United States.

Other titles in this series:

Gravity keeps us on the ground,

Magnets can move things all around.

We use pulling and pushing
for games and swings,

And birds push down on air with wings.

Forces keep us in motion
and slow us down,

Without forces, there'd
be nothing around!

What happens when your
bedroom door gets stuck?

**You might have to
force it open!**

When you force something,
you make it do
what you want it to do.

Has your mom ever forced
you to clean your room?
Or wash the breakfast dishes?
Or take your pet lizard for a walk?

(Bet she's never had to force you
to eat ice cream for dinner!)

There are other kinds of force, too.
There are forces that make us stick to Earth.
There are forces that make your
soccer ball fly into a goal.

There are forces that make
your soccer ball roll to
a stop before it even
gets to the goal!

Have you ever
jumped off a chair?

Have you ever jumped
off a sidewalk?

Have you ever jumped
out of a tree?

**(Don't jump
out of trees!)**

6

When you jump,
do you fall up or down?

You fall down because of gravity!

Everything in the world is held to Earth because of gravity.

Gravity is a force. It's the most important force in the world!

If gravity got turned off—which can never happen—our cars, pet lizards, picnic tables, and everything else would zoom away.

DANGER
LAB SPACE

Nat

Gravity is the force that holds everything together!

What else holds things together?

When you put pictures on your refrigerator,
you use a magnet to make them stick.

Magnetism is another force.

Magnets can
attract or
repel each other.

Every magnet has a north pole and a south pole.

If a north pole and a north pole are put together, they
repel each other and move farther away.

Have fun playing with two magnets!

» What kinds of things can you pick up with them?

» Is there anything you can't pick up with the magnets?

» What happens when you put the ends of the magnets together?

» What happens if you switch one of the ends around?

TRY THIS!

If a north pole and a south pole are put together, they **attract each other and move closer together**.

When you and your friends
have a tug of war, you are
all using forces on the rope!

One team creates a pulling force
going one way, while the other team
creates a pulling force going the other way.

Who wins the tug of war game? **Whoever can make the strongest force!**

What happens if both teams make
equal forces on the rope?

Does the rope move?

Does anyone win the game?

Forces can be pulling forces.
There are also pushing forces.

When you push your little sister
on a swing, you are using a force
to make her go higher and higher.

**And higher, and
higher, and higher.**

TOO HIGH!

What happens when the swing swings down? **Better watch out!**

The swing—and your sister— can use a pushing force on you if you're in their path.

When you ride a bicycle, what makes the wheels move?
You are using a pushing force on the pedals, which
makes a pushing force on the wheels. Your
wheels move on the ground and send you
riding your bike across the pavement.

What happens if you lift up your feet and
stop pedaling? You might glide for a while.
Especially if you're going downhill!

But eventually, your bike will stop.
You will stop. What makes you stop?
Another force!

A force called friction makes
the bike stop. Friction happens
when things rub against each other.
The bike wheels rubbing against the
pavement makes the bike slow down and stop.

Forces are what keep us on the ground, make us move, and stop us from moving forever!

Be on the lookout for forces all around you!

GLOSSARY

attract: to pull together.

force: a push or pull that changes an object's motion. A force also means to make someone do something.

friction: a force that slows down objects when they rub against each other.

glide: to move smoothly.

gravity: a force that pulls all objects to the earth.

magnet: something that attracts metal.

magnetism: the force that attracts or repels between magnets.

pulling force: a force that pulls something toward you.

pushing force: a force that pushes something away from you.

repel: to push away.